THE DEED OF GOD

The Deed of God

by JOHN W. LYNCH

Copy 1

SHEED AND WARD - NEW YORK

© SHEED & WARD, INC. 1961

LIBRARY OF CONGRESS CATALOG CARD NUMBER 61-11790

NIHIL OBSTAT:
THOMAS COSTELLO
CENSOR DEPUTATUS
FEBRUARY 11, 1961

IMPRIMATUR:
✠ WALTER A. FOERY
BISHOP OF SYRACUSE
FEBRUARY 12, 1961

MANUFACTURED IN THE UNITED STATES OF AMERICA

Let him easter in us, be a dayspring to the dimness of us, be a crimson-cresseted east.

GERARD MANLEY HOPKINS, S.J.*

* From *The Poems of Gerard Manley Hopkins* (New York: Oxford University Press, 1937).

FOREWORD

The total **DEED OF GOD** includes everything that is, or ever was, or shall be, sin alone excepted. However, the narrative which follows here traces God's thirty-three years of human life, the three years of His public speech, the three hours of His Calvary pain, the three days of burial, as He willed this great Redemptive mystery to repeat and remain, *from the rising of the sun to the going down thereof,* within His Mass, given in the Name of the Trinity —Father, Son, and Holy Ghost.

Words printed in italics, whether within the lines or separately, are all exact quotations from the Douay version of the Bible.

The facts asserted in the Third Section are based on the authority of Father J. A. Jungmann, S.J., in his *The Mass of the Roman Rite* (New York: Benziger Bros., 1955). The liturgy had developed by over two hundred additional years in the era of Hildebrand, but on pages 85 through 90 I have used the privilege of foreshortening in the interest of a compact narrative.

J. W. L.

I

Let us be here freshly, suddenly,
With nothing of tradition in our eyes;
No German pine trees cut triangular,
No Polish cookies, sugared, spiced,
No plums in puddings, walnut marmalades,
New England farmyards quilted with the snow,
No gifts, or voices, or the ribbons thrown
To tangled piles of sweet confusions.

Let us be here suddenly.

> *And the earth was void and empty, and
> darkness was on the face of the deep.*

Until her fingers lingered on His form,
Felt the beating breast, the hands, the spine. . . .

She cried, then, cried to Joseph. . . .

11

Lambs huddled, and their thighs were crouched
Beneath them; quiet, sprawling sheep
Were witnesses in curled humility.
An ox spread out against her woolen shawl,
But when she lifted Him and looked . . .
She need not, at this virgin moment, weep
The portent in these mute, appropriate
Companions, manger-cousins in a cave

Laid in a careful corner, held
By slats on wrappings she had bound,
He breathed so purposely our air
That thin and hollow straws could move
To Infant lips like timbers sought, caressed.

Shepherds rustling on an outer rock
Made new defenses of her arms in fear
That afterward subsided to a calm
At good invasion. Over her the hosts
The shepherds told brought winged assisting minds
For adoration, and their spilling arc
Gave singing complement to all her stars.

The night, reluctant at Divinity,
Had learned His first, His human cry,
Did not falter, kept commanded course,

And in the morning dawned Him to a road
That will be winding, turning past the towns,
The shores, the deserts, through our crowded streets,
Through meadows, over waters, down the lanes
Until the road discovers that it held
A last intended purpose, and must find
The end His feet were seeking on a hill.

A law inscribed by Moses gave detailed
Direction for initial paths,
And now a young girl with no speech
Of His or sound for guidance, scarce a month
From birthing Him, enfolds Him in her arms,
And like an emissary come of all
The deep, accumulated Israel years,
Envoy, herald from the total trend
Of prophecy, brings Him to an old
Appointed place, and locks Him to His first
Achievement of design.

                    Not to relatives
Or neighbors as a mother with a Child,
Not sweetly proud, not shyly with her Own
Taking easy smiles, and not to any warmth
Or nursery.

Her steps are moving down
Our dust, treading cobbles in the streets
Of David, mounting stones of Solomon,
Crossing courtyards, gracing marbles, seeking,
Seeking one place, one place, only one. . . .

With turtledoves and Joseph's falling coins
For sign, she holds Him, Victim, to the roofs
Of sacrifice, and here surrenders Him!

Stones remained upon the stones, flames
Still flickered on the wicks, pillars stood,

The veil within the Temple swung unripped,
And on these walls no tremors came to shake
The vaulted roofs, and yet a prophet voice
That cried to Israel six hundred years
Before, might now be wakened sob to break
The silence and to tell of ended time.

> *Behold the Lord whom you seek . . . shall come.*
> *. . . and he shall purify the sons of Levi . . . shall*
> *refine them as gold and as silver.*

Simeon petitioned at her gown,
And if we recognize his sign of peace,

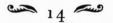

Perceive the deep content that covered him
And bedded Simeon for death, we feel
The halt, the brief reluctance in this voice
Announcing revelation, and to her the road
Of one day waiting, still to be endured.

> *Behold this child is set for the fall and for the
> resurrection of many in Israel. . . . and thy own
> soul a sword shall pierce. . . .*

Did now the shading of a pillar streak
Across the courtyard as a cross? Were tapers
Now an April noon, the golden roof,
A sky, the walls, horizons for a world?
Were slippered feet the tread of Roman boots?
The chanted psalms, resounding, clamored shouts?
This street, these stairs, a spattered, staggered hill?

Behold this child, this speech of Simeon
Become in her His words, *behold thy son?*

As utter gift accepts all consequence,
As waves are humble to demanding tides,
As buds consenting to a spring assent
To autumn, she might know . . . and long ago had felt
The spear within her young, resistless heart.

But now with fact outspoken, plain and clear,
She stands beneath the moment of her new
Annunciation, not by Gabriel,
But by Simeon.

     She bends to take her Child,
Her Child, while whispers of her first consent,
Echo and repeat until her arms are willed
To be the wooden beams, her near caress,
The lash. Her glances now are plaited thorns.
She sings to Him the baying of the mobs;
Her kiss is promised clink of treachery.

All cups hereafter that her hands will brew
Are brimmed with vinegar and gall; the robes
She looms are scorning for a Fool; His feet
Will be forever sandaled with the nails;
His face despised with spittle, and His sleep
Will be the first immaculate death.

Across the vast adventure on our crust
Of earth, stars and timbers, swelling springs,
Have seemed so worthy we have given them
The name, the tribute that is God's, but now
An embassy from farther dark moves near
In rolling, tasseled caravan.

We call them kings, tradition counts them three,
Debate so leisurely of origins,
Of routes, that we have counted to ourselves
Unnecessary tales when all we need
To touch their obvious significance
Is insight Matthew traces on his page.

These Magi from the Orient are priests.
Like eager, seeking strangers they have hushed
Barbaric prayers, abandoned altars built
Beneath Chaldean moons; they seek for One
Whose Name, Whose purpose they had always sought.

Where is He? We have come . . . .

Thrusting in their hearts lies unappeased
By words, and fallen back, unsatisfied,
Drives out for more, for more to give them lunge
And impact at the barriers of space,
Of time that closes like a leaden room.

Gold is gleaming on the knotted floor,
The sleepy night is fragrant in the cone
Of incense. Tribute is, the very dust
And gesture of a priesthood, prologue, sign,
Adornment for its hand, and afterward
The liquid lapping from a casque of myrrh
Is gift to mothers when their sons have died.

His chosen road that at the very last
Will swing across the chaos of our dark
To bridge the chasms, be a cable-web
We cling to over unimaginable falls,
Turns, and by a Herod's jealousy,
Traverses deserts in a fear, escapes
The clang, the flashing of the swords, turns
And finds direction at a pathless Nile.

He keeps His sanctuary at her young
Embracing arms and weary Egypt looks
Unknowingly upon a Pharaoh come
Constructing life, and spurning tombs,
Unknowingly accepts the hidden God
Whose parody and twisted image spread
Above the sands. He is a Child
Who in a morning plays upon the ground
Where Isis gleams, but in an afternoon
Runs confident to warm receptive knees.

Herod died, and then a dream of home
Is sent to Joseph, who uphoists the Child
Above firm shoulders, walks in lengthened stride
Along a laughing trinity's return.

Calm considerations in her eyes
Give Joseph pause, and pose a further thought

Of Bethlehem. Should Bethlehem be home?
Should avenues of ease be made to slabs
Of sacrifice? Or ready access fall
Before Him to the Temple roofs? His place
Be here, a neighbor to Jerusalem?

Herod died, then dreams of warmer home
Envelop Joseph, and the name of home,
Son-given and against all worried plans,
Is Nazareth.

      The Will that sent Him here
Breathes quietude on Nazareth, a place
Assigned for Deity to be a Son
And know a human way.

        The kitchen bench
Stands tall before Him; fingers learn to lace
A sandal, cling to Joseph's hand; His speech
Increases, tutored of an accent heard
While they are speaking; phrases fall from Him
That light His mother's eyes to laughter; jars
And spoons are implements in childhood's play.

He learns the safety of a grassy ground
That is His own, the refuge of a door

Should sudden showers come; His face is tanned
By sun, and cooled by wind; His hair is smoothed
Maternally.

When cousins come, the forms
Of games are offered for His eager choice.
His legs grow sturdier, autumns fall
With fruits full ripened. Bark upon a trunk
Gives exquisite exploring.

And when the years
Revolve and crusts are kneaded, birthday sings
Above Him in a gay, good festival;
Birthday then was birthday for a Child.

He will be moulded to us, made our own
By pain and by betrayals. He will sink
Beneath an anguish, rise identified
And *one with sin*, and in Him all our days
Will multiply and dig against His hands,
His feet and heart, the signature, the sign
Of our deserving. Brotherhood will fork
Him to a cross. Yet for some moments here,
The Will that sent Him, summons quiet joy

Around Him for a hidden space of peace,
That He might know a rooftree and a home.

———⌣———

Now is the pilgrim road: caravans,
That for millennia had rocked and creaked
Through tented dust, careen and sway in weighted
Memory of Moses and the split
Of the rescuing sea. Another year had turned
In time, another year, another year,
And Israel, remembering, makes way,
Camps and clusters at the Temple gates,
Crusts the altars in the blood of lambs,
Reswears a covenant, resuscitates,
Sings anew a future in the psalms.

From Galilee they come, from Bersabee,
Out of Naim, from Bethsaida, from Dan,
Walking down from Cana, Magdala;
Another year has turned, another year,
And somewhere in their scattered caravans,
Anonymous and unattended, hid
Beneath the grooming of His deep intent,
Jerusalem gives entrance to the Boy.

Scholars must not over-urge the theme,
Interpret, spindle fancy, try to see
Beyond the given narrative of Luke. . . .
But still this springtime of His first release
From childhood, first of cleavage in the held
Sweet secrecy of Nazareth, reveals
Him near a destiny that even now
Is sure, accepted, chosen in abrupt
Repeating of the day she carried Him.

He walks upon the paths of David, seeks
The honest altars, stands so young beneath
The roof of Aaron . . . and His journey ends
At place whose meaning is a gift to God,
In a week whose victims are the Paschal lambs!

Rituals of Seder supper done,
Prayers all capped and cantored, tales retold
Of history, then Israel returns
In caravans that trail and hope along
The road, at last, to leave Him here, alone.

He lingers, sleeps beneath a night that folds
Across Jerusalem, to wait on dawn
When young eyes, searching, mark the light that slants
Across the batten of the Temple walls?
And more? The cobbled streets where Roman hooves

Strike smoky sparks in legion arrogance?
Centurions? A balcony, a court
Of judgment? Scents on winds from Olivet?
Sandals wander toward Gethsemane?
Or does He cloister in a lonely watch,
And listening to lessons droned once more,
Another year, another year, in time,
Keep limit for Himself at hidden porch
And archway, corridor, this little Boy
Among the Pharisees who must have known
The nearness of maturity?

We are certain only that her triple span
Of anguish ended in maternal cry. . . .
Three days for her of more than Calvary. . . .
He rose to them and said:

Did you not know
I must be about my Father's business?

Cry out, John, be a voice to wilderness.
Make straight His paths, for now the slow
Preliminary roads are at an end,

His feet are swift, directions sure, the dust
Is rising from the thongs you would not loose,
The hill He seeks lies only over time
Diminished to a span of numbered days.
He bends to water pouring from your hands,
You hear from Heaven tenancy,
Watch the signal of the wheeling Dove,
Cry out, John, be a voice to wilderness.

His pathway seeks the sea-less, grateful rocks;
He pauses, lost to prayer; the desert sun
Burns dry Gethsemanes against His flesh,
Satan sifts Him, searches by a sieve
Of lies, to fail before commands that make
Of Satan, chaff.

              Tall against the sky
He comes in masculine return. The path
That hid beneath a prostrate prayer, moves on.
Cry out, John, be a voice to wilderness.
Give Name, announcement, speak Identity.
Male and female we are spilt to races,
Scattered over continents and down
The yawns of time. We wait, John, give Him Name.

*Behold the Lamb of God. Behold Him who taketh
away the sin of the world.*

Soon the road finds other feet to tread
Behind Him, and so soon His single speech
Is: *Follow me*. Young John, Nathaniel,
Simon, Andrew, Philip, James have left
The Jordan pebbles; here on a widened strand
They are first to meet the summoning
That is, with albed and cinctured multitudes
To show where skies will run the blood-red wine,
And all the mornings break on death-white bread.

He hastens, moves with them to purposes
He keeps in Galilee, and when a house
In Cana welcomes them for festival,
They suddenly discover they are guests,
That joy around them brims to marriage feast.

This is her own, His first
Foretelling, and as wine
Is spilling, copious from spouting jars,
Their hearts *believe in Him,* and now
Unwittingly a steward speaks for her:
But thou hast kept the good wine until now.

Past Capharnaum, Tiberias,
Clustered lakeside towns, until the call
A season brings rolls out to Israel,

And He, for His second last observance, comes
To Temple doors, surveys the cluttered courts.

Not now the Boy of twelve: He is the Man.

> *My house shall be called the house of prayer; but*
> *you have made it a den of thieves.*

Wrath like Sinai flames within His eyes,
Tips the tables, slashes, scatters coins. . . .

> *And as Moses lifted up the serpent in the desert,*
> *so must the Son of man be lifted up: that whoso-*
> *ever believeth in Him . . . may have life eternal.*

Since multitudes had harvest at His hands
Grown of the meager loaves, since they had fed
On fish that schooled and flickered in the nets
Miraculous He cast because of love,
And afterward had watched the baskets fill
With crumbs, they shouted that He must be king.

He turned to hide away, but they perceived
He had dispatched vocationed fishermen
Across the lake, yet somehow followed them
On pathways tracked above obedient waves.

It was enough, and as they huddled, wet
Above pursuing keels, the murmurs ran
About the wondrous year He yielded them.
He had spoken with authority,
Cast out the devils, raised a widow's son,
Healed the leper, sat with publicans,
Of how He must be king for now their tongues
Had savored food. . . .

       They found Him, cried aloud,
And found (Capharnaum!) they must accept
Another bread.

     Lord, give us always this bread.

Then speech engraves an iron dialogue
Between His purpose and refusals made
Of meaner measuring; we feel
The first emergence of His vaster plan
That in a year will find fulfillment drawn
At table in Melchisedech's design.

> *I am the living bread which came down from*
> *heaven . . . He that cometh to me shall never*
> *hunger . . . he that believeth in me shall never*
> *thirst.*

They argue Him His ancestry, exchange
Among themselves the damaging and plain
Descent from parents they had well assessed.
Yet no relenting softens in His eyes,
No pause for explanation, no retreat,
And having led them to the linen's hem
Of mystery, bids their hands come in
And with majestic certainty invites
To the golden paten.

> *I am the living bread. . . . If any man eat of this*
> *bread, he shall live forever: and the bread that I*
> *will give is my flesh, for the life of the world.*

Bethlehem denotes a house of bread.
Their fathers had the manna from the feet
Of Moses, and their lingered lipping taste
Had moistened to His given loaves, but now
Against His urgency, against the drive,
The deep propulsion of His word, they pose
Their caution in a thin, retreating silence,
Ask Him how, what manner? Can this be?

He spends a breath, He summons solemn oath,
His voice rolls on superlative to worlds.

Except you eat the flesh of the Son of man and drink his blood, you shall not have life in you.

Simon and the others had observed
An empty place that imperceptibly
Increased around Him. Then He stood alone,
With nothing more to say, no more of vast
Endowments, chalices, but only now
A simple question uttered to them all.

Will you also go away?

Simon was a voice that did not fail
To pour a total wisdom from his heart.

Lord, to whom shall we go? . . . We have believed and have known that thou art the Christ, the Son of God.

Days thereafter were adventures lived
So swiftly Twelve could neither count nor guess
If months or eons fell between His words,
And when it was His will to bring an end
To words, yet all about them they could feel
The swelling enmity above the plea,
The hunger of His poor. He bade a man

Lift up a sickbed . . . on the Sabbath day!
He cried: You know of me and whence I am,
Until the sullen silence and the stone
Hostility of stares had gone beyond
A mere resentment, had become a speech
Exchanged in patterns of a definite
Resolve which more and more was growing plan
That censure of His words, His act, must cease.

Simon heard another question posed
Above a lengthened, various confusion.
Once more he bluntly answered: *Thou art the Christ
The Son of God,* and when reward of praise
And blessing ended, Simon's fingers closed
On keys of jurisdiction, and his name
Solidified for distant centuries.
Then it was that Peter also heard
The faint dim consequences of the plots,
The fixing of the pattern in all lives.

> *The Son of man must suffer many things . . . be
> rejected . . . by the high priests and the scribes . . .
> be killed . . . . !*

Peter could endure no more,
And groping in the tumult of a shocked

Bewildered mind, he seized upon a shout
Of protest, and was bold enough to cast
It outward in rebellious love, until
The same Voice that had tied him to the white,
Long primacy lashed in such rebuke
He stood afraid, but even then this Voice,
Encircling futures and the hidden, dark
Expectancy above remaining road,
Did not relent, or cease, or seek a theme
For easier disguising, and they heard,
For the first time heard, insistently and plain
With sternness blunted to ambitions,
For the first time, what His Father's Will enclosed.

> *If any man will come after me, let him*
> *deny himself and take up his cross and*
> *follow me.*

The path that now has little more to thread,
Mounted Tabor, paused before the flash,
The searing of Divinity set free.
A blinding moment shed the shades of flesh,
And Peter, prone upon the ground in awe,
Cried out for leave to build memorials
Against forgetfulness. The Vision dimmed,
The shadows of Incarnate closed and held.

Earth regained old skies, the ashen suns.

The only answer was His word resaid
Of pain, of death they could not understand;
And in their hearts *they were afraid to ask.* . . .

In distant, locked Jerusalem
Torches burning in a secret room
Set deep within the Temple made a play
Of mottled shadows on the faces leaned
In circle for a conference. They sought
Rebuttal for a grave where Lazarus
Had listened too obediently for ease.

Dead men come alive are evidence?
Sufficient? Even may be set against
Authority of nation, place, prestige?
What now to do? What answer to a tomb
That stirs and smoothes the wrinkled wrap of death?

Caiaphas stood tall beneath the gleam
Of torches, and in glittered arrogance
Rebuked uncertain shadows, while his eyes
Were bits to deeply drill imperatives.
When he spoke, he spoke not as a man
Ungowned, unmitered, stranger to the robes
Of Aaron or the ephod sleeve. The tone

Resounding to the Temple was the theme
Of Israel.

> *It is expedient for you that one man should die*
> *for the people. . . .*

In Galilee a silence weighed
Upon the air. Nowhere on a road
Could crowds assemble for the seeding speech
That scattered in a sower's fling
The lilies of His care, the hundredfold
Of yield that came of reckless listening,
For He had gone away, and rumors held
That He had pulled a desert's distance down,
And in its caves, companioned by the Twelve,
Lay closed within the prudence of a prayer.

Until the signal of a swelling moon
Brought springtime buds, the summons for a Pasch
Awaited since adventuring began.

Jerusalem already watched at streets,
At entrances, and when the news was sure,
He had not dared to come, command went forth
That first and merest sight of Him be made
A matter of report.

In Galilee the prudence of His prayer,
The secrecy were ended, and He strode
Before them like a chieftain summoning
A faint, discouraged rabble to assault.
Beyond the gates of Ephraim He turned
To southward, past the hills, beyond the wells,
The pastures and the greening fields
Ahead of them with Peter, James and John,
The others trailing in a ragged rout
Until He turned to utter prophecy.

> *Behold we go up to Jerusalem, and the Son of*
> *man shall be betrayed to the chief priests and to*
> *the scribes and ancients. And they shall condemn*
> *him to death and shall deliver him to the Gen-*
> *tiles. And they shall mock him . . . spit on him . . .*
> *scourge him . . . kill him . . . !*

Under curves of April sky
In glooms and shades, beneath expectant sun
That is to darken on the quaking day,
He wills to be the Man, with arms upraised,
With worship in His wounds, and in His eyes.

> The worship first,
> By purpose thonged in Him

Of stronger bond
Than sinews to His body's bone.

The worship first
Our need of tribute recognized
By fall of blood
Before the Father's yielding Will.

The worship first
In offered Gift that still must be
For Sovereignty
And full submission's marrying.

Then the grief,
By knowledge that is deep in Him
For bitter taste
Of chalices our sorrows make.

The grief,
The somber sum of what we did
By day, by night,
In angry impulse satisfied.

The grief
For deeds and for the lack of deeds
That bruise His mind
In wounding that is pain unhealed.

Then the thanks
By knowledge that is welled in Him
For honeyed taste
Of all the giving. . . .

Thanks
For total sum of all we hold
By day, by night,
Our firelight, food, our life.

Petition now
Against the loneliness
Outside His heart,
In all decision past His heart.

Petition now
For wife, for child, for friends,
For grain, for fruit,
For foaling in our fertile fields.

Petition now
For deeper want, for worried need,
In urgency. . . .

How many times since Childhood had His feet
Pressed human imprints on receiving dust
To lure caressing winds and leave a part

Of earth remembering and envious
That they had blown away? What estimate
And sum of mercy's errands, or the steps
That paused to tell a parable, and then
Moved on by other journeys to the blind?

Recount them now, include His path across
The waters of Genesareth, the first
Few tottering attempts beyond the wrist
His mother loosed to let Him go, the tread
That crushed the shavings in a shop, that walked
To Martha's oven, pushed a shore of grief
For Magdalen's acceptance till He bade
Her lift her head and find His drying eyes.
Let nothing pass, lose not the faintest, least
Impress of Him upon our earth, for now
His steps are ending, and a thousand more,
Intensified, must bring Him to the hill
Where troops will wrench His dusty sandals off
To shoe Him with a nail.

The Temple stands in darkness to the moon,
Midnight streets are echoing with sound
Of His diminished company, for one
Among them is not here, is fled away
To honors and to coins that had conspired.

Olive trees are bending for an arch
Of murmurous inviting entrances
But He has paused beneath their porticoes
To let His mind turn to the ancient words
Isaias sadly wrote upon a page
That in this moment is no longer script
Or prophecy or writing held apart
By years and generations. He is here,
Erect and tall, with all delaying done
Against the pain, the tears. He is a Man
Despised, a Man of Sorrows, struck,
A leper wounded for iniquity,
Afflicted, bruised for sin, the price of peace
Upon Him, but no sightliness nor love.

He does not move, He opens not His mouth,
And, staring at the fate Isaias penned,
He reads the deep perdition He must be.

With the wicked was He reckoned.

Stillness falls, olive trees
Are bending in an arch of entrances;
He shudders, sighs, He stoops beneath the boughs.

Who measures at a mind in pain
Engages in a useless folly, comes

To no arithmetic and trials dreams;
Who stretches tape across a loneliness
Makes survey of the Pleiades with skeins,
Constricts the reaching heavens to a patch;
Who tries to weigh an anguish, reads
Uncalibrated, dizzied scales.

We own no compass for the stricken soul
Nor any plummet at the wells of guilt.

A catafalque of trees is company
In whispered dirge above His friendless dark;
Then sound of sobbing comes, a broken moan
That neither boughs, nor leaves, nor centuries
May deaden, and our hearts, appalled,
Search out the lesser meanings of His cries.
We seek the consolation of a sob
Compelled of merely nails, impending thorns
Envisioned now to penetrate His veins.

We crouch at mean appraisals; His endured
Gethsemane is lessened by our quake,
Our cowered fear. This is a vocal shame
As loathing now Himself, the Innocent,
Outreaching to the instant face of God,
Is one with sin. He faints beneath the dark
Identity He wills to be His own.

Not spikes struck in His feet, but slime across
His soul; not spittle and the whine of whips,
But inward swarmings and the viscid trail
The sludgy evils draw, as when a stone,
Too long against the earth, is turned to light;
Not jagged wounds, but scabs exuding stench
In pustules, till a sickness writhes in Him
And He is prone upon the rocks with blood
Oozed outward for dishonors at His mind.
He twists with penalties for being Man,
And wrenched from Him, twin pleas for pity fling . . .
One to His Father that He need not drain
This deepened draught . . . and one for absent friends.

Hours of agony extend, endure;
Trees are stilled, the moon seeks denser veils;
Birds are silent: only sound of long,
Too labored breathing drags beneath the dark,
And in the breathing, words that are a Will
Unchanged, submissive, knead Him more and more
Within the mould of us until His time
Is ended, and He staggers up to meet
Our kiss, be truly us, our Own.

Rome commanded. . . . lines of orderly
Efficient companies had marched

In squares of stiffened lances on a swift
Return from nonsense: tread of boots
Is competent to roads. And yet the loom
Of indecision tangles under trees.

Exchange and parrying of words,
Dim figures fleeing to the shadows, swords
Circle as a boy runs naked to the wind . . .
But now the Caesar order is obeyed.

Legions, not of angels, form a guard.
Inexorably the key of time has turned
In the latch of prophecy, and fated names,
Long hidden in the secrets of the years,
Are clear forever. Faces are defined
That had been vague; over Him they swell,
To swim like large eventful planets come
To baleful confluence above the hours,
And out of all the years the face
Of Annas is the first.

        The house of Annas
Glows within this night; he stands,
He wears upon him both the legacy
And robes of Aaron. Annas, royal priest
In Israel, and by a recognized,

Authentic lineage permitting him
The threshold of the Holy Place, presides
At swift, initial acts that issue forth
Our destiny and his. So when the tread
Of soldiery is echoed at his door,
Annas has devised a needle probe
Of questions: he awaits an answering.

> *In secret I have spoken nothing. Why asketh*
> *thou me? Ask those who have heard. . . .*

Annas probes no more: a knuckled fist
Obedient to gesture cracks for him
Complete rebuttal, and a spurt of blood
Is trickling at the Lips the fist had bruised.

> *Answereth thou the high priest so?*

Across the cobbled pavement Caiaphas
Had not relied on vesting of prestige
To bring solution, and he moves within
A gathered council heavy in the weight
Of plans, and confident that witnesses
Compelled from sleepy beds are adequate
To pour his hot intent within a cast
Of cooling verdict. Suddenly the buzz

Of speculation blurs, and Caiaphas,
Swift turning to an opened door, observes
The blood already on His mouth, the mark
This Annas left in hint before their minds.

Caiaphas could pray for nothing more
Except that consummation quickly close
Upon inaugurals, and with a sign
Too artful of abundant mercy, asks
For silence and for evidence.
But witnesses are tangles made of knots
And ravels, and a pattern is confused
That should be sewn along a plain design.
Consummation does not quite ensue.
In subtle council Caiaphas detects
The mien of legal pain. Formality
Is at an end, and in the priesthood's pride,
Caiaphas has risen as a harsh,
Brocaded advocate who will be heard,
And will be heard precisely on the point.

> *I adjure thee by the living God that thou tell
> us if thou be the Christ the Son of God.*

He looks to the waiting faces, He is tall;
Under Him His planets burn, His stars.

I am.

The High Priest tears his vestment for the first
Of signals that will soon be made complete
In split and ripping of the Temple veil.
They bleat: *He's guilty of death.* They brawl.
What further need have we of witnesses?
They surge outpouring to the morning streets
In haste to Pilate, seeking Caesar's noose.

Pilate's face
Is leaner than the rest, a cynical,
Taut, leather mask of little confidence
In anything but native wit, and yet
He loves enough of justice to regret
The lack of it entirely.

Think not meanly of this Roman scene
Of justice shrunken to the barren forms;
Compulsions wrought of Providence are here
In everlasting, public irony.
This show of caution yields to us the full
Unfolding of the meanings in His Name,
Moves the moment of His final steps
To sequences where Love may tell Itself
Divinely in a last extravagance.

Neglect the first, the tentative
Quick question in this Pilate's speech,
The scorn for truth, his skeptical contempt . . .
Save that an answer ringing in the brief
Laconic dialogue cries out: *I am a King,*
And *"I . . . give testimony to the truth."*

Neglect the politician's strategy
That sought another's judging . . . save that now
A fourth face rises as the leprous moon
Of Herod's countenance peers down on Him
With fleshy gaze above obsequious
Delight since Pilate still observes the rights
And happy honors due to Galilee.

Neglect the whole preliminary fall
Of lesser rhythms for crescendo comes
In thunder, and the April day is cleared
Of all digression, rolls into a theme
So simple, so insistent that the mind
Must hear, compelled to follow to the end,
And even after centuries, must still
Endure. Herod has returned Him now,
Old issues hold, and Pilate is once more
Involved. Within his conscience justice pleads
What evil hath he done? Barabbas grins

And is no answer; water in a dish
Is useless gesture; voices, echoes, grate
Against the judgment seat. They cry for death,
Insisting spatter of His blood be theirs
To wear and be a badge upon the skins
Of children; they demand and will not cease. . . .

Till Pilate's scruples seize upon a scheme
Of mercy, and command goes forth to lift
The Roman whips from places where they coil.

Warm complicity of pleasure spreads
Across the courtyard and the tumult sinks
To silence as they turn with swarming eyes
Anticipating, measuring His form,
The virile suppleness of limb,
His back, His shoulders broad beneath a gown.

He stands before a blunted post . . . He stoops. . . .

Can time be counted over pain? Is space
Between the biting of one lash, and when
It curls with lick of fire, eternity,
Or only waiting? Are the moments locked
And linked and bolted in a stippled cage
Where neither breath, nor end, nor surcease comes
Releasing lattices and stopping screams?

How long the cobra welts encircling legs,
His shackled arms, the quiver of His thighs?

Nowhere on the careful record's page
That notes all other hours, all incidents,
Is guess or stricken whisper of this time.
We have a sentence written, then no more.

Except that afterward
A new adornment mocked His head with thorns.
Purple robing fell,
Gesture in the soldiers' scornful knees,
A stool for Him to sit on,
Scepter made of tall, thin withered weeds.

Pilate's face
Is leaner than the rest, a cynical,
Taut, leather mask of lessened hope
In anything but Caesar's will, and yet
He loved enough of justice to regret.

And now before his final verdict falls,
Before the cry comes that will be a threat
Of tales to Caesar, here before he yields
Or earns a name within the changeless creed,
Before command goes forth to choose a cross
Among all other crosses for the death

Of God, this limited, restricted trace
Of virtue in him finds a balcony
And offers him as spokesman to the world.

These peoples are mature to destiny;
Their steps have now gone far enough for them
To know the road they walked was not the path
Of the world's old wanderings, but was a course
That had no end or purpose save themselves,
In witness to a Will that had been fixed
Since Abraham, their father, first received
The burden of Intention for his seed.
They are assembled, they are gathered here
From every meadow of their labored land,
And over them the Temple's stones are huge
With towering on slopes that David chose.

Melchisedech of Salem, priest and king,
Had been a name long chanted in the psalms.
Familiar with the altars where the feast
Of Moses falls at dusk, they had been Law,
Correction, guidance to our race, a clue. . . .

But by an inner vision of the soul,
Behold how more than Israel is here.
Legions, Greeks, the dark Numidian slaves,

Medes and Parthians, Cretes and Elamites,
The whole tumultuous throng of all of us
In generations deep and reaching back
To Adam, clustered, upright, outward spread
We touch the very epilogues of time.

And somewhere, hidden here, a face unknown,
Unrecognized, is like the face of one
Who huddled to his breast a fairest lamb
And laid it at an altar on a hill.

Pilate sees the purple cloak, the scars,
The thorns that leave no comeliness in Him,
Commands Him to a ledge above our years.
And with a language deeper than his words,
Pilate cries to men and history:

   Behold the man!

Skies received Him like a signature,
And for the term of three accepted hours,

Kept neither north, nor south, nor east, nor west,
But only feet impaled, a wounded head,
The thrust along His arms to bleeding hands.

He is formed, and nailed and vised to final frame,
A brace to hold against the outer Press
Of Being closing on our nothingness
To crush so utterly that any race
Might weep dishonors in fecundity.
He is Noah and this wood is ark,
His suspirations are as desperate doves
Seeking tops of Sinai for us all.
Here He is, spread above His hill
To lift against the lunging of the world
His firm, concentric caliper that draws
All time and all horizons in, forever.

Golgotha is cluttered with the tools
Of cruelty; boots of soldiers scrape
Against the rock where waves of shouting rise
In skirl of triumph. Screaming rips the throats
Of thieves, and then an answering applause
Is loud beneath their writhing.
Contention argues ownership of rags
As priests are laughing at the throw of dice;
They sneer, they stride amid the fevered crowds

To stir a new excitement, when a voice,
High pitched and shrill upon a single string,
Whines upward in its summary and theme.

> *Thou that destroyest the temple of God and in*
> *three days dost rebuild it . . . . come down . . . .*

His body is a bleeding calm, a wound
Of moveless majesty with no reply.
Silence wraps Him and above the earth,
In space to sight as distances of stars,
He wills to wait, to live this little while.

Moments wheel beneath a darkening sun,
And in a hush of air the frightened birds
Are stilled beneath the pallid day, too soon.
His hands pour deeper wells, His arms are wet
With lingered crimson, slower breathing comes,
While they who stand upon the altar of His hill,
Have heard the long forgiveness fall from Him
As though He were an Advocate and Plea.
His judgment at a last confessing heart
Is murmured, words are said that give His own,
His mother, wider Bethlehems, and now
The shadow of His dialed Purposes
Is closing, closing to the final line

That had been set and drawn upon its rim
Since time had known the future of this hour.

He lifts His head, and from the clotted wood
Becomes a Victim Who, at last, presides.

His Will is His, and of His Will begins
The formal liturgy for This, His Deed.
His Wisdom searches down enfolded pasts,
Seeks syllables that Israel might hear
For full avowal and for destiny.
His vision fixes now upon the day
Of David; He cries His antiphon:

My God, my God, why hast thou forsaken me?

Silence follows, yet His voice
Has hammered echo everlastingly
That time may now be anvil for the words
He summons to His death but leaves unsaid.

I am a worm and no man:
The reproach of men and the outcast of the
people.
All they that saw me have laughed me to scorn:

They have spoken with the lips and wagged the
head . . . .
For thou art he that has drawn me out of the
womb:
My hope from the breasts of my mother. . . .
They parted my garments amongst them:
And upon my vesture they cast lots. . . .
They have dug my hands and feet.
They have numbered all my bones.

The stroke against His circled shadowing
Is closing, slowly closing to the line
That had been set and drawn upon its edge;
His heartbeats now are numbered to the lance
That soon will search to find no numbers more;
His breast is rising, sinking, and His throat
Is dried like a potsherd made of clay, His tongue
Cleaves to His palate. Yet His Will is His,
And of His Will He sobs out to fulfill:

    I thirst.

No more, no residue, no more of pain,
Nor width, inclusion, no more task to wait
Until the clear appointed slant of time
Reveals; no more of yearning in the gulf

Of earth, and in its deep foundations now
The quaking shudder of a triumph starts.
He lifts His head, the love upon His face
Shuts out the splendor of resisting day . . . .

It is consummated.

As one Who of His own Will chooses sleep,
He bows His head upon His breast. He dies.

II

His FACE AT center of the framing wood
Stiffened to the ancient, rigid mask
Abel wore to wring the cry of Cain.

Submissive, bowed, His head conferred consent
To thrust of final wound, and twisting down,
His legs became as drained autumnal vines.

When staring eyes no longer mirrored vast
Horizons, did not answer to the dusk
Of era's end, shudders in the rocks
Commanded skies that thicker dark might wrap
Around Him for a shamed, concealing shroud.

Quaking rolled, cleaved fissures in the hill,
Increased, split louder, ran beneath the last
Confessions of a stunned centurion,
Cracked upward, outward, troubled graves, until
The thunder shuddered to the Temple door.

Walls were sudden surfaces to sound,
Courts were echoes, stairs were cannonades,
Upper chambers, halls, high corridors
Trembled like a rampart under siege,
But when the stagger of the earthquake ceased,
The soft concealing of the Temple veil
Still hid the secrets of a Holy Place.

Folds of purple, falls of opulence,
Weaves and threading in the thick brocade
Still waited, waited, when a violence,
A rough disruption, ripped as from a harsh
Relentless hand; then in a silken scream
Astonished folds split wide; the severed halves
Swung free. The inner, golden floor
Stretched naked to the vision of the world.

Upon the hill a silence, calm,
Contrasting, wedged an interval between
A time forever ended and a time
Just now begun. Tumult ebbed, crowds
Receded, soldiers wheeled to make report;
A man named Joseph hurried with a plea
To Pilate, and against recovering skies
The Body that was Joseph's argued claim
Forked in dark resemblance to the beams.

How much accomplished worship here?
How much of adoration? Floods
Of blood more potent than a drop?
What wound, which laceration yields the most?
Which nail, the one within His hand?
Which pain for us best competent,
Redemptive to our helpless orphanage?

How much of sorrow turned in Him
Who, sinless, cast Himself to sin?
How many evils written here
Are white and in His red, forgivable?
What injustice, cruelty,
What lust, what loves that should have been,
What chill, infertile winterings
Are warmed away by breath no longer breathed?

How much of gratitude is poured
For us from His emptied, beakered heart?
By sagging head, by welted knees,
By water dripping in His wound like blood?
Thanks for harvest, thanks for spring?
For mercies, for the grant of time?

Petition spreads along the arms
Stretched out, where, pulled to permanence

They keep His gesture by decree of nails.
How much petition, what the prayer,
The argument, the urgency of this?
How violent? Enough to bear
Away all kingdoms He had told in words!

But now the mind must turn, abandoning
Attempt at contemplation, and in awe,
No longer striving at a sum our thoughts
Can neither measure nor enclose, must make
Reversal, see all moments and events,
Not in sequence of historic time
Advancing, but as time that is a wheel
Compliant to His mastery of Will.

Falling from His form thin shadows make
Suggestion, point us downward, lead us back
Through streets and courtyards, under olive trees,
Until, like ancients seeking in a past,
Unfolding, tracing purpose and intent,
We leave the summit of His Friday's cross
To mount the stairway of His Thursday's room.

The room is empty now. Shadows close
About a table where no candles burn
Above a waiting cup. No bread is laid

To linen, and expectancy that once
Had looked so eagerly that pause in speech
Or gesture of His hand were like an age
Above the gathered Twelve, is gone. The night
Does not now quiver to His sound of words.

Doors are shuttered; darkness holds no flame.

Yet John had been here, all the chosen faces
Leaned along these couches, and these walls
Had taken them in sanctuary set
Since startled stars looked down on Bethlehem.

Peter, James, Bartholomew, the rest . . .
Watched here while familiar Seder feast
Unfolded in ancestral ritual,
And when competing questions rose of rank,
Of honor, He had stooped beneath their feet
With towel and basin in rebuking hands.

Whispers sighed within His quickened speech
About betrayal; and a motion made
Above a dish sent Judas to the streets
To inventory coins and scheme a kiss.

Quiet, and an unstaccato loan
Of time had made this little borrowed room

So intimate, so cloistered to the world
They felt they were aloof from time and one
With Him in permanence. No distance now,
No separation, and their lingered eyes
Had found in His responses promising
Inclusion closer than ambitious hope
Could guess at or conceive. His fingers reached;
He blessed: He broke His bread; He gave to them,
And consummations hinted on the shore
Genesareth were so fulfilled that awe
Compulsive in them would not let them breathe
Or think the shore endured, or any place
Beyond this room, this Love to mutual lives.

Take ye and eat. This is my body.

They knew. By evidence of silenced seas,
By winds that calmed, by Lazarus who plucked
With fingers at the underside of shrouds,
They knew. They knew effect, not wondering
That sight was blindness, form, a frantic fraud,
That weight was but His own obscurity.

Taught by Him before the Word was word,
Answering with hunger, they consumed.

Wine within His cup awaited them
In more than Cana's poured festivity;
Then flowed of Him Who willed to be the Vine.

Drink ye all of this; this is my blood.

Here within this room a new command
Rose stronger on His voice than they had heard
Controlling substances already meek
And instantly obedient. Mere bread,
Mere wine bend humbly in His universe
And own no liberty. They are but furrows,
Vineyards, harvests, ripening and flow,
And need no conquest other than the first
That threw them where a void had been, and cast
Created seasons for their sunlit use.

A larger mastery is moving now,
More subtle purpose, worthier command.
His voice in summons speaks of human lives,
Of futures, and a transformation comes,
Not to simple fruitage of the earth,
But to our race and on our potency
To worship in Him as He worships God.

He gloves them with His living hands, stretches
His length of fingers for their own; He wills

To be within them as a breath for words,
Enunciates with men His syllables;
He carves their faces to His own design,
Engraves identity; He presses down,
He moulds, and in an instant, other Christs
Recline around this table as He sees
His own eyes looking back to Him from theirs.

Do this for a commemoration of me.

Again the concept in the mind must turn
Surmounting time and time's deceiving fall.
Calvary is ended, but we now
May see the patterns of the full event
Combine, perceive that here before His cross,
His deeper revelation had appeared.

Quiet violence was in this room
Where white of linen spread a crimson stain.
Whips were biting, whips unheard, nails
Were piercing, subtle nails, arms were spread;
The beam above His thorns, already fixed,
Had lifted up unseen; His vertical,
Unyielding altar was this table, flat
For supper. Candles burned within a dark;
Stairs already had become a hill.

And when we watched Him here with minds that search,
We could have heard full meaning of His words:

This is my body . . . which is given for you. . . .

Wine was arteried and dripped within
The golden Golgotha of gleaming cup.
Wounds bled in its depth and at the rim
A pulse poured endlessly a torrent Love.
Here within this room, O we who see
Athwart the finished deed of Calvary,
The probing of the soldier's final spear
Was needless. Listening we could have heard:

*This is my blood . . . which shall be shed for
many unto remission of sins. . . .*

Here where living breath had phrased His words,
Death lay; His altar was bequeathed.

Somewhere, somewhere in this Friday's night,
His priests, new priests embraced our common way,
With year succeeding year, with nothing more
Of clarity to futures than the heart
Can glean by hazarding at dubious straws
Retrieved for evidence. We do not know

What roof they sought, and on the record's page
Their names are absent.

                            Only women went
To wash His wounding and to mourn before
The place where wrappings were not swaddling clothes.

Hands ordained are empty; purposes
He sealed within their touch, sleep unresolved.
They raised no bread, poured no chalice wine,
And death that even at a distance hung
Against them like a body's weight, had seemed
Conclusion and not summons to a dawn.

Thomas added nails to spear and found
A simple logic; Peter could regret
Surrendered sword, and even John who heard
His heartbeat louder than the hammer's sound,
Must judge the hammer victor. Pentecost,
And winds and flung horizons still are hid
In time; Emmaus and His second crumbs
Of signature had not been given them.

Within this night they mourn and are but men
Who dreamed His words were echoes in a dream.

We must not pity, must not now conclude
They heard Him poorly, or that memory,
Needing to survive a merest span
Of hours, had meanly failed, for they were men,
But scattered men, and in our lives we hug
Long lessons in the school of lighted years.
Crosses, unmistakably, are signs
Inwoven on our bended chasubles,
Ropes are cinctures, thundering is bells,
The baying of a crowd, our murmured prayer.
And we have seen too long the lifted Host,
The separating cup of mystic death,
Not now to know, beneath deep silences,
That Pilate's cry was true. We strike our breasts,
We kneel and summon sorrows to our minds,
And over mornings, priesthood-mornings, plead
Behold the Man!

     But they knew only sleep
On failure's bed, with hissing whips for hope,
With futures shattered in the sound of nails,
While out beneath the night a Paschal moon
Fingered what He carried on this day.

III

Word-sower Paul, who scattered Christ
Along so many roads, so many fields,
Who furrowed Corinth, reaped at Antioch,
Paul, who plucked at Athens' weedy stones,
Broke the winter of his prison doors,
Made urgency a day of summer rain;
Paul already was a history.

So when at Troas the assembly, shaped
By previous visit, filled an upper room
To break the bread, they knew this eucharist
Would once again be framed by speech of Him
Who gave it *on the night He was betrayed.*

Day had vanished to indifferent seas;
Lamps were burning, salt, warm breezes blew
The curtains inward toward a table laid
With loaves, and with another cup that stood

In memory. They were attentive, hushed,
And over glances marking women's care
For linens at the sacred place, they knew
Whatever scoring words their Paul had flung
At Corinth, words of failure, bitter blame
For wantonness, need not be uttered here.

> *For as often as you shall eat this bread,* he wrote,
> *and drink this chalice, you shall show the death*
> *of the Lord. . . . Therefore, whosoever shall eat*
> *this bread, or drink . . . unworthily, shall be*
> *guilty of the body and the blood of the Lord.*

Corinthians reformed, and penitent at anger cast
Protectively about this central Deed,
Had understood anew that heritage
And meaning, spread now by the Spirit's wing,
Lodged among them for a nail-less cross,
Must be perceived and guarded in an awe,
In wider charity resembling His
Who summons to the tables of His death.

Jerusalem, steadfast house to house,
Communicating in the broken bread,
Kept rituals already definite,
While neither Matthew yet, nor Mark nor Luke

Had written gospels down in words. So here
At Troas in the April night, a past
Could rise and make with Paul a dialogue.

He strode among them but he was not tall
Save by stature of his towered speech.
They heard; they could not be content again
With smaller speech. His voice pronounced a fire.
His thesis: resurrection and a Life
That fountained, coursed and dug His way in men
Surrendered to His vigor. He is real
For Greek, for Jew and Gentile; is within,
Is over, pulsed, enveloping; is strong
Beneath new destiny. . . . O were there years
Or long repeating seasons given him,
Not merely moments snatched before farewell,
He, Paul, *the least apostle,* could not then
Exhaust that plenitude. . . .

                    Yet eloquence
Was but a preface in the Troas night,
Preparation for His Suppertime.

> *Thou art worthy, O Lord our God, to receive
> glory and honor and power. Because Thou hast
> created all things.*

And for Thy will they were and have been created.

In eager answer, wet expectant eyes
Held thirsting to the chalice, told the bread
Their hungering. It did not matter now
That Paul was Paul, *Word-sower,* harvest-tongued.
Titus might be here, or Timothy,
Barnabas, or Silas, even one
At Troas who would seek no foreign seas;
It did not matter, for when Paul had ceased,
Set his priest hands at the table's edge,
Paul became anonymous,
And *doing this* had no more countenance
Or name, or posture, attitude, no self,
Or signature, or voice, but *put on Christ,*
Stitched and gowned himself in Christ, took breath
Of Christ, lived by heartbeat not his own,
Shed his body for the Other's form.

Silence folded, deep and strong,
Silence made a temple in the night.

"The Lord be with you."

          "And with thy spirit."

"Lift up your hearts."

"We lift them to the Lord."

"Give thanks unto the Lord."

"It is meet, and just, and right."

"Fitting now indeed,"
And then his arms impulsively apart,
In spread as though embracing them, Paul prayed
With cadences that caught the ache of all
Their yearning, and aroused in them new needs
Like hidden pulses under secret selves.

Not yet the stable form, the matrix shape
Of discipline that will be liturgy;
Not yet the preface, canon, and a prayer
In words so fixed they will not ever change
Or be submissive to a sentiment;
Not yet the dignity, the Roman coin
To mintage for the soul . . . but improvised,
A plea composed of urging and a breath
Blown warmly from the mind, strophes made
Of impulse, near necessities, a face
Beloved, and then, remembering:

Who art in Heaven, hallowed be Thy name.
Thy kingdom come. Thy will be done. . . .

In chorus, murmuring beneath the lamps
Of Troas, phrasings rolled that Christ had taught
Among beatitudes. Then signal fell
From's Paul's intenser eyes, and they were stilled.

Silence folded, deep and strong,
Silence built a temple in the night.

Bread was lifted in his steady hand.

This is my body.

The deep-cupped goblet tipped with waiting wine.

This is the chalice of my blood.

One by one they came from time,
Bent here still beneath the hold of time;
Fed on food, took within them drink,
That till the world's end is above all time.

Worship first
By Bread that is not bread,

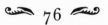

76

But stronger bond
Than sinews to their body's bone.

Worship first,
By wine that is not wine,
But pour of Love
Within a Blood now satisfied.

Worship first
By Deed of praise that they have made
To Sovereignty
And in submission's Offering.

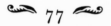

Then the grief
He had given them to lift
Beyond the flow
Of acrid tears their failures make.

Then the grief
In total sum of what He did

By day, by night,
In double Deed that is but one.

Then the grief
For sins, for stubborn, thorny guilt
To cut His flesh
In wounding that was Love revealed.

Then the thanks
In knowledge that is welled in them
By winey drops
Of full appeasement He had shed.

Then the thanks
For gift within their children's lives
That heals their wants
Permitting sleep, uncompromised.

Then the thanks
For being here around His cup

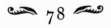

And for this Death
That in them now is veining life.

Petition still
Against the shroud of loneliness
Apart from Him
And on all pavements far from Him.

Petition still
For wife, for child, for human hands,
For peace on earth,
For daily need He did not scorn.

Petition still
For final aid at final day
When He shall be
Unveiled of bread, unsigned of wine.

Silence folded, deep and warm,
Silence at a table in the night.

Pliny the Younger, Legate of Bithynia,
Politician,
Minor spider on an empire's web,
About the year one hundred thirteen,
Pulled a parchment forward with official quill
To let his frigid Emperor understand
The conscious zeal that Pliny had
In making numerous arrests.

The letter still exists; and when we scan
The Latin paragraphs,
We read how he enquired, examined, fixed
Undoubtedly, established as a fact
That some, whose name was Christian, rose at dawn
To hold among themselves a sacred feast,
A meeting of such consequence to a God
Called Christ, they stubbornly refused
A Legate's counsel to desist.

In other matters, in all other forms,
He, Pliny, Legate of Bithynia,
Found them quite amenable.

Yet in this single, secret rite, for oaths,
For mutual avowal in their ranks,
Even threat of death could not avail!

Another parchment now, precisely creased,
Catalogued among an archive's file
By number, author, style, antiquity,
Subject for the plates of photostats,
Can seine across our river-view of time
And give us, suddenly, a cause to stare
At breathing brothers.

Justin left this evidence,
Justin, born at Flavia Neapolis,
Pagan till he learned of Christ,
Justin, layman, unordained,
Who wore no sacerdotal robes, yet died
In the bloody vestment of the Calvary priest.

His paragraphs are quiet, calm, aloof
Sufficiently to seem but plain report.

"The bread and a cup of water and wine mixed are
brought to the one presiding over the brethren; and
this food is known among us as the eucharist. No one
may partake unless he is convinced . . . and is cleansed
in the bath of baptism."

This, as Justin carefully describes,
Is done at Rome . . . Rome where Peter rowed
To make an end of fishing when he hung
On the crossed, inverted hook . . . Rome
Where Paul concluded all he had to say,
Then stretched his neck beneath the sword of silence . . .
Rome of Cletus, Linus . . . Rome, before
The catacombs . . . where Nero's Jews
Were blamed in the ancient lie . . . Rome, the center,
    fixed.

Yet outward, in periphery flung far
By the inland sea, this food is also known
As eucharist, and ceaseless words of prayer
Are whispered in the same deep meaning.
Altars rise in Alexandria,
At Smyrna, under Asian skies, along
The rims of Syracuse, identical
And clear of purpose intertwined to one

Intent; and Polycarp who saw the face
Of John might visit Rome, be asked,
Even by a Pope, to take the cup,
The bread, offer in his own design.

"Only here does all creation meet,"
Irenaeus cries, "only here
In Christ is all creation lifted up
And sacrificed."

But now an urgency,
Hesitant in search for formula,
For text imposed, no longer improvised,
Is swelling in the certitude and flow
Of days, observed in cresting, seeking flood
And firm direction, when a name appears
Of one who pleaded for a frame of law
And reticence. Hippolytus, the priest,
Calls out in Rome that symmetry be shaped
About an Act that had been multiplied
By all the turnings of three hundred years!

But still no answer. Antioch and Spain,
Ambrose, Chrysostom, the Gallic meadows,
Celtic islands on the farthest tides,

Are matching ceremonials to catch
The native genius. Genuflections bend
Profoundly, matin sound of chanting stirs,
Vestments are restitched to Gothic cut,
Country saints inspire commemoration,
All is living, flowing to the Deed,
Embroidering the colors and the threads
Of many cultures, till the stone of Rome,
Plummeting of law, traditions' weight,
Another Peter's presence, O a need
For universals meet, and Rome instructs.

Somewhere in these hidden days a man
Whose name our scholars cannot find, sat down
To write, composing, using double turns,
We note, of language in his style, and when
He rose, anonymous, the canon's form,
Enduring ever since, was in the world!

Time had silted centuries on Paul
And Troas, buried Corinth, and the need

To learn Whose death beseeches Deity
From bread and wine. Time had thickened, set,
Gowned and tamed the Goth, the Visigoth,
Brought scimitars to Africa, to Spain,
Bequeathed the Lombard crown, sent Charlemagne
To empire with the wisdom of his schools,
Till time stood gravid of a thousand years.

Gregory from Cluny was the Pope.

What grey basilica he chose, what day,
What hour for festival could not arouse
Astonishment at Rome, and as his word
Had spread, they found it usual, aware
The Pope would journey out of Lateran
Majestically for public eucharist.

In morning wind, before the day
Had wrinkled under marshes' heat, they filed
From all their seven hills in populous,
Engrossed procession. Silver crosses led,
Silver crosses shafting up the glints
Of ancient honor till their singing march
Fell silent, and they entered through the arch
Of Mary Major.

Along the legions' streets, accustomed pomp
And manner sent the pairs of acolytes
To walk a vanguard; then the guardians
Of written treasure in the sacred books;
Then deacons, vested, mounted, holding rein
On horses lest they prance beyond a line
To mar the stately gait; then Gregory,
Alone; behind him household troops, the ranks
Of purpled servitors; but Gregory,
Alone.

His thoughts, his meditations now?
His theme before this people's sacrifice?
Did he regret his cloister's empty cell,
Remembering he had been Hildebrand,
The monk, free to silence, free to hood,
When he had not been Gregory the Pope?
See within his heart the corridor
To Cluny's altar where his sandals trod
A solitude?

Or did his pace recall
Temerities of Berengar who swore,
Regardless of the testament of years,
That bread could not regive the living Christ,
Nor wine, the blood of Christ, Berengar,

Whom Gregory in iron word condemned,
Summoned to a Council that condemned?

Suddenly the formal walls loomed near;
Procession in the morning mud had paused.

He prayed: and in him Christendom had prayed.

Beneath the portal's curve, a lifted alb
Descends, scarves are tied across his shoulders,
Dalmatics sleeve his arms, cascading comes
In fall of bell-shaped chasuble.
When Gregory had bent submissive head,
Accepting collar made of fairest wool,
His thoughts flocked back to John: and to the Lamb.

He reaches for his maniple and waves
It in a formal notice; clerics kneel
With seven torches; incense billows prayer;
Somewhere in the throng a chorus swells:
"Rejoice ye in the Lord!"

                    They attend him,
Escort by ritual accorded kings.
He moves among the Romans . . . aisled by tiers
Of faces . . . past the homages of priests,

Past prelates . . . past the bishops . . . till he sees . . .
His altar is a table unadorned,
Raised upon a marble dais, plain,
Waiting for another Suppertime.

Torches separate, and one by one,
With all the splendid train and retinue
In order, following, they form a ring
Of reverence. Gregory ascends,
Salutes the table, kisses on its stone
The symbol cross. They bow to him, unroll
A carpet gorgeously. Their breath is held
As soaring chant is stilled, for Gregory
Has stretched his body, prostrate, on the floor.
He rises, bends, and then the Kyries
Beseeching mercies wail contrition's cry
Until the Pontiff strides to Peter's chair,
Bids that silence be. He sings:
"Gloria in excelsis Deo. Gloria."
He faces to the east and at the end
Of choiring, hears consent of the throng's "Amen."

A page of Paul is read aloud; a page
Of Matthew, breached for kissing, has received
More solemn deference, and when the words

Conclude, the books, silk wrapped, are sent
With guardians to vaults of Lateran.

A chalice now is brought by priestly hands,
Is centered at the table as the Pope
With love and purpose, stern of countenance,
Delays all movement till in linen folds
A corporal spreads his altar, end to end.

The full assembly needs no other sign.
Their step is quiet as they make approach.
Like men who tread upon a path to Christ,
Like children coming with permitted gifts,
They carry in their hands an offered bread,
Bring within their fingers vials of wine.

Two little loaves, new-baked at Lateran,
Nest in Gregory's palms, and when he leaves
His throne, intent in silence, they await
Until the formal postures of the priests
Are rigid patterns. Liturgy is paused;
They see now Gregory alone.

His speech is murmuring the canon's prayer.
Attentively they listen waiting words
That have been sounding through the thousand years,

To fall commanding on the bread, to cast
The bread away; to summon over wine
In call of swift surrendering.

Gregory has raised accomplished Host;
Archdeacon's hands assist him with the Cup.
Courtesy is offered, kiss of peace
Bestowed beneath wide Mary Major's roof.
Content, subdued, they lengthen straight,
Slow, shuffling lines that will advance, retreat,
Reform, advance new-ranked until the last
Of opened mouths is fed the Bread He is,
Unfailing Wine reviving them to Life.

Gregory upon his throne has kept
A space of prayer. What more for him
To do, what more to say, except to move
Among them, blessing them, in slow return
To where less loving issues core his mind?

Not suddenly, or with a leap
Of subtle excellence, stones arise

From the springtime ground of Christendom,
Or summoned by a royal whim.

(Cologne and Canterbury, Rheims,
Laon and Lincoln, Senlis, Wells.
The aisles of Chartres, the doors of Notre
Dame.)

Not by persuasion, not design
Conceived in individual plan
For small supremacy, nor were
These columns piled by arrogance.

(Beauvais and Tours, Amiens, Sens,
Westminster, Le Mans, Saint Mark's;
The aisles of Chartres, the doors of Notre
Dame.)

But out of seeds that Paul had sown
To germination in the rain
Of years, of common fertile loam
Breeding stalks thrust towers to the sky.

(Saint Stephen's, Durham, Angoulême,
Mont Saint Michel, Toledo, Treves.)

A people said:

"Take arc and curve, enclose the light
By wide lace spaces in the wall,
Dig down to rock, but let the eyes
Look upward where the columns rise."

A people's children said:

"Carve devil, angels, chisel saints,
Blend the colors, bubble glass,
Let granite lines that are concealed
Be gracious as the hands, the face."

A people's children's children said:

"Weave tapestry and thread brocades,
Illumine missal, spin the gold,
Implant a martyr's bones for slab
To be His table in His house.

Yet leave unsigned, anonymous;
Cut in no claim or signature,
Permit no title, own no fame
Around our trifles offered Him.

His windows here are nothing more
Than form and structure He may use
When teeming from our common cribs
We come tumultuous and one."

(Cologne and Canterbury, Rheims,
Laon and Lincoln, Senlis, Wells;
The aisles of Chartres, the doors of Notre
Dame.)

Thomas of Aquino, massive, friend
Of Bonaventure, cowled Dominican,
Feels the God-gift, flesh, around his soul,
And so considers he is not a soul
Alone, but man.

Accepting that, respecting body's cause,
Counting five to be the avenues
His senses give him to an outward world,
Thomas dips his pen, begins to seek
Reality.

His life becomes a contemplation,
Lucid in the shaft of reasoning,
Uncluttered by all issue save the truth.

Universities at Paris, Rome,
At Naples, swoop like eagles at a ledge
To hear. Popes and Councils summon him.

But when his thought is weary, reason slowed,
Thomas heaves his questing bulk to stand
In silence, waiting, with his head against
A tabernacle door.

      A kindred mind
      Trusting light
Taught in the marble dark of Greece,
      Groped and touched
      The shadowed air,
Peered in the pantheon dark of Greece.
      Traced a scroll
      Consecutive
Wrote in the glimmer-dark of Greece.

And now in the century of inheritance,
William of Moerbeke, fellow in the schools,

Translated faithfully the ancient script,
And Thomas had his Aristotle plain.

> O not to take
> And then baptize
> The light that speared the dark of Greece,
> Not accept
> Or borrow now
> Of nothing purer than the light of Greece,
> But moulding, fusing elder verities
> With newer: making Aristotle serve
> The cause of Christ.

This dialectic of the substances,
Of matter and the forms of matter, place
And time, of shape and outward circumstance. . . .
This whole analysis of what is in itself
And what is accidental . . . Thomas saw,
And, index to intelligence, saw more. . . .

It was a language, alphabet and term
For spelling out in quick philosophy
What Christ, Creator, and the Man Divine
Achieved by one controlling of His Will!

The substance of His Body takes a form
That, save for what He willed, is alien;

A whiteness, weight, a texture not His own,
But bread's; not color and the flow of Blood,
But now a liquid in the taste of wine;
To let, by God's august, transferring word
A Deed that is memorial be Deed
In total Calvary-repeating Act!

Thomas, poet, on his knees has cried:

"Sing O tongue His glory,
Sing His body, sing.

Sing O tongue His blood,
Sing His gift for all.

Born for us and given us
Of her who clothed Him in her womb.

Sing O tongue the night He left
His life of sorrow with His gift.

Himself He gave, O sing, O sing,
Himself by word to bread and wine.

Behold the Host and let depart
All ancient rites to newer grace.

Sing O tongue for senses fail
Beneath the faith that sees Him so.

Let praise and jubilation be,
Sing the Father, sing the Son,
Sing the Holy Spirit,
Sing, O sing. Amen."

So many noons had stroked the Medici
To insolence and ease, so many heirs
Regarded splendor at the evening fall
Of fountains, strolled beneath the cypress trees
Discussing Raphael's line, Cellini's thin,
Reflected subtlety, Rome could not hear
Thunders rolling through the Rhineland crags,
Nor feel the chill storm fracturing the world.

So much of confidence, composite years
In firm estate, delays at Avignon,
The strength Agnolo made conspicuous
In dome, on Sistine wall, the temporal weight

And lull of long possession, hung on Rome
In fog so palpable a Pope could say
The sever of the lightning, and the whine
Of wind told nothing but a monk's dispute.

Luther nailed his theses to a door.

Then barons came, the small competing kings
Of sly intrigue, adventurers at courts
For marriage, landgraves, dukes, alliances
By earls, and they could estimate the plan's
Increase at chaos while their eyes grew large
With looking at the monastery herds,
The acres of the schools, and down the broad
Inheritance accruing to the Deed.

More than Luther hammered at the door.

Trent assembled, wearily.

Eighteen years, three Popes, some war and much
Diplomacy, a plague, adjournment, calls

To readdress confusion, bishops, priests,
Calm cardinals are here engulfed by time
Till Borromeo stood to mark the end,
And knew that Trent had cast anathema
With language like a blare of trumpeting
Against dark dissolution, had retained
The past that Trent had gathered to affirm.

We need not quiver to the massive sound
Of symphony that counterpointed Trent . . .
The statement, harmony, crescendo, crash
Of full renewal in the synod theme
And affirmation by a final chord. . .

Listen now. The Thirteenth Session. Hear!

> "If anyone deny
> That in this Eucharist,
> Most holy, most revered,
> So ancient, so adored,
> Is Body, Blood, and total Christ,
>
> Then: let him be condemned."

Hark to the Twenty-second Session. Hear!

"If anyone deny,
That on this altar
Deed is truly raised
He died to give
By this unbloody cross,

Then: let him be condemned."

A swift few centuries since Trent have heard,
And turned, as we have turned, to hear again
The staturing, the size; and yet the sound
Is only music from the ancient years,
And if our living line of melody
Can reach to tombs: then in the tombs they sing!

They who sailed to green San Salvador
Never knew the masted fleet had touched
Not India, but a world. Yet it was there.
Fresh wind blowing, coasts and inland seas
So great that cataracts, like brooks between

The forest and the mountains, washed a new
Horizon to the earth where men could walk,
And still before them keep horizons more
To scan. The Spaniards came, the Portuguese,
The French, and with them, undismayed, the priest
In scuffed Assisi sandals, in the black
Ignatian robe, adventured farther spaces,
Raised His cup above two continents.

Measured time is futile beat at Rome
Beyond the dialing of hours from Tierce
To altar, thence to Vespers and the quilt
Of Compline pulled across the guarded night
Till Matins, and another dew.

Calendars achieve significance
Only under feasts and ferials;
By seasons hurrying from purple fasts
Of Advent, lingered antiphons, to time
Set free again in the new, white Infancy;

By myrrh and incense and the Magi gold;
Septuagesima, Sexagesima, Lenten crusts,
His lilies trumpeting the broken tomb;
Red for flames; green for summer's hope. . . .
Yet over Rome the running years
May chime together, link within a name,
Fugue to decades, be Pontificate.

We speak of the time of Leo, time
Of Boniface . . . in chronicles enmeshed
With history in a world unsecular.

Giuseppe Sarto,
Son of the postman at Riese,
Caught the eye of the parish priest,
Received instruction, and at age
Thought suitable, achieved his First Communion.

Afterward some Latin and consent
Within the school at Padua
Admitted him to tonsure, and the fire
That burned before him in the Spirit's plan.

At twenty-three his hands first knew
Their chalicing, and in his voice now,

O unbelievably, O holding tears,
Were syllables that let him give to Christ
The cross that was the same cross, yet his own.

Tombolo. Treviso, Salzano,
The children, (mornings!) journeys to the sick.
His pulpit, (mornings!) oils upon the old.
To Mantua in miter,
Venice then, and cardinal.

But when the white cloak fell across his soul
Of white, when keys were in his hands, the white
Host waiting for a child's white heart
Became in him a purpose fired of dreams.

Not two years passed and first decree
Commended daily Bread; not three,
Until the sick were set exempt
And free to take Him as the Good Physician.
Seven years of Sarto as a Pope
Proclaimed to earth no knowledge more need be
Than a child's perceiving Christ is here
And not the common, crusted bread.

Giuseppe Sarto sanctified his time,

And Pontiff of the frequent Eucharist,
Made his the era of the sweet return.

Eugenio,
Son of the old nobility at Rome,
Dressed by birth for courtliness,
Entered as a right the subtle ranks
That keep the bluntness of the world from edge
That could destroy.
And as the vote fell, and a conclave ceased,
Lofted on a balcony, a voice
Pronouncing, carried round the world:
"Annuntio . . . habemus Papam . . . Eugenio. . . ."

Responsive roaring at the central place,
By Trajan's column and great Agnolo's roof,
Rang welcomes on electric pulse
To men as far away as hemispheres.

When shattered nations faltered in a slash
Of steel, when missiles, screaming, buried towns,
Another Pius rising on the wheel of time
Walked in a garden, pondering, alone.
Amid diplomacies and reasoned pleas,
With failures crumbling on the threat of more,
His mind turned to the Deed that did not fail.

Eugenio ruled that law be minimal,
And summoned men to come, to kneel, to eat,
To multiply the Deed for peace: today!

IV

TODAY,
Or any day,
Light slants sharply to Atlantic tides
For sad illumination; only waves
Of grey and seething precipices slide
To fogs, to glints, to penetrating rains
Like first accomplishment of Genesis.
No islands, nothing of the land or men,
Or homes, or testaments of living loves,
Only hiss and cresting of the spray,
The curving, raucous cries of ceaseless gulls,
Until the edge of day that had been flung
Of continents strikes the flinty cliffs
Of high Quebec.

                 Quebec is crag first brushed
By cassocks, rock where once the frozen hands
Dug deep the sockets for the candles' butt

Before they raised a roof against the snow.
Here the dawn-light falls familiarly
To move the quiet nuns on, one by one,
Assembling for their wintry trellises
Of chant around His Deed. And as the day
Sweeps past the river, touches little towns,
Saint-named and nested under watchful spires,
His Deed repeats, repeats. . . .

Manhattan strutting to the sea endures
Assault, and with the thrust of granite arms
Upraised in pagan protest stubbornly,
Defends against invasion of the dawn,
To wince before the day's swift subtle light
On slabs and cornices, and on the streets
Where dew-wind seeks and whips along the curbs.
Dust and papers spin, the sky is new
Above steep angles in the masonry,
Trucks begin their grinding, slatted crates
Are slammed to pavement doors, and in the earth
The thunders gather to reverberate
An iron frequency.

But spread across
The City, like a refuge and relief,
Like acres gardened, multiplied to keep

Significance, like silence in a roar
Of sound, like white achievement set amid
The neon striving, all the sanctuaries
Waken from the shadows . . . beg His love.
Taper wax-flame touches waiting tips
Of candles, and the morning's meaning lifts
From dawn until the dawn ends in the noon.

Insistently and clear beneath these windowed
Teeming citadels, His Will is not
A thinning, lonely wedge against neglect,
A singular, half-desperate attempt. . . .
Guarded cloisters, polished convents crush
Between the shoulders of the crowding walls,
Chapels kneel behind a market place,
Saint Francis shields two levels of a church
Beneath his monastery that is shelved
And ribbed and alcoved with a hundred altars;
Cinctured monks feed Christ to multitudes.

Cathedral gothic dwindles in the press
Surrounding it with planes and parapets
Of lofted stone and Rockefeller bronze.
Schools make corners, parishes, a stoop
Abutting to the traffic's snarl,
A college huddles in a alleyway,

 111

And everywhere (O avenues!) the Deed
Embraces measures of the daily pain,
The joys, the quick, the wrung petitions of a throng.

Blocked, embedded here and girdered square,
The City's bulk takes grip in rigid hold,
Builds the vast and piled geometry
In huge compulsion down to the ocean edge.

Yet, threading through when light falls from the east,
Hidden arteries of worship run
Beneath the blunted bulk to vein and branch
His sacramental, seeking sanctities.
Printers, homeward on cemented lanes,
Find Him when the night has hardly gone;
Watchmen stop before a holy place;
Subways spill a crowd that has observed
How wide a moment scurrying affords
For kneeling, and in neighborhoods the old,
The ordered meeting of the Deed with dawn
Advances; teachers pray, and here before
Their classes learn of Him; lawyers come,
The poor, the debonair, the derelict,
And when the press of enterprise has slowed,
When time has swiftly wheeled and has besieged
The margin that must end His Deed, then clerks

Postpone the ledgers, flee from offices,
Fasting, meet Him in the city's noon.

Thrown far above horizon's speeding arc,
The dawn now lights the slumbered continents
Where land sprawls in a spread four climates wide.

Bells ring glad renewal, hands are poised
Above His chalices, bread is laid
Against the paten, and the words repeat
That hold His ancient, red, remembering
Until the risen sound, the whisperings,
So sigh along the altared hemisphere,
That continents are sibilant, and all
The day is roused, and eloquent of Him!

Chancels of the Argentine are gold,
And Mexico is shrine of hammered silver.
Jewels gleam, the silk lies shimmering;
Wood is satined, polychrome is bold
Against a ceiling. Thick brocades are hung
With laces, webs in Aztec fabric, shawls
Make woven legacies . . . for Latin love
Is uttered in a shout, and does not yield
To reticence, but sings in symphony
The lesson of the spikenard and the hair.

These are beginnings, prefaces to vast
Profusion, and the light keeps tenure here
For huge inaugural. Beneath the light,
As multiplied as villages and hills,
As usual as roads and ordered to a constancy,
Expected, normal, known, enduring now
In lingered ritual, the Deed moves out
Across our western land.

                    A boy along
A street is hastening to sacristy
Where surplices are hung upon a wall;
A priest drives thorns within his mind to feel
Fraternity; vestibules are wide
To early steps of women, cars are curbed,
Freshened linens fold, unfold, refold
Within the day for liturgy and plea;
Chalices are standing in a line
Like grails; a campus at an orchard's edge
Kneels down in pattern, and novitiates
Are hushed for gowning's hopefulness.

Today,
Or any day,
The old observances at death are new.

So summon now our lonely courtesies,
Embrace the stricken, warm the words by tears,
Send our flowers to the moment's need,
Form processions, sadly speak a name,
But still confess our ancient impotence.

This is end, conclusion, and a birth
That woke once to a promise, is undone.
This boxed and carted figure was a man.

Full decades are processioned now, his hopes
And plans, his struggles in the restless dreams
That answered to ambition, and the wounds
Of being tender and alive to loss.

This is the weight and body of a man.

But as he lies, concealed and separate
Beside the bended knees, then we are sure:

More than breathed, polite formality,
Much more than even honest grief now folds
About him for the broken Host is raised
Against *his* need, *his* chalice is fulfilled,
And in the broad assemblies of the dead,
We leave him not anonymous and lost,
But under light that gives him requiem
And clear identity at Golgotha.

Pacific blue rolls swollen in the full
Horizon's round and makes a moving world
Where brief successive islands rise to meet
The eastward wind bending lonely palms
Like acolytes for far confiteors.

Candles now have lost the circumstance
Of home and burn in victories above
The scented grasses, and the formal tongue
Of Latin speaks amid a languid air.
Gothic yields to stretches of bamboo,
Sanctus bells are ringing to a wash

Of surf unceasing since the silences
First sounded in the first created tides.

Sunrise flaming in the tropic dawn
Raises brazen canopies for Him,
Hangs light to vast reredos in the sky.
Here He is, and has been; long ago
Balboa's wake drew lines across these seas. . . .

In huts at leper places, in the arch
And doming of cathedrals made to vault
A Spaniard's hope and memory of home,
Behind Dutch harbors, past the teak, the spice,
Along lagoons and at the end of paths
Hacked beneath a jungle . . . He is here. . . .

Yet we must pause in counting now among
These scattered faces of the ocean lands
To mark the island that is like a cinder.
Iwo Jima, difficult to chart,
Is stark with memory of beaches,
Recalling agony of boys who scratched
Across its inner rocks with hands, to leave
Their twenty-thousand bodies graved in sands.

A shellhole, cavern under splintered steel,
Made sanctuary, and artillery box

Gave altar to the chaliced charities.
Priest-hands leveled in a Deed of pain,
Vestments twisted in the ashen wind,
Kneeling boys made walls of human shoulders,
Lest the priest, or chalice or the Host
Be harmed. Searching now we must remember?

We need not name nor knowledge of the banns,
Nor see their shy eyes' eagerness to know
In some new-fenced and British town in far
Australia, two will rise to stand before
Their love, join their bodies to His Own
For nuptial that weds the heart in Christ
Beyond the pledging two alone could swear.

They are not held to laces, and the ache
Of gesture, nor to ribbons on the sprigs
Of purposed leaves, for when they meld their lives,
Cast their love together at the years,
When out of two they fuse one bravery,

They meet first in the union of His flesh,
Speak beneath the rooftree of His cross.

India, indwelling in a dream
That God lies dreaming in a dream of dreams,
Looks out beyond the dawn in reverie,
Brooding to a muffled, moveless time.
The Deed here is an edge, a severance
To full releasing, and the nave is filled
At Rangpur, Goa, Kashmir, and Bombay.
Stately bishops walk cathedral aisles,
Schools keep vigil at a missal page,
Xavier's brothers, teaching, are at home.

Then light becomes a flood above the plains
And valleys deepened in the tread of men
Beyond all memory, where hills are numb
With tribes and races, where the dust has borne
The beat of nomad wandering so long
That bone and blood lie kindred to the ground,
And Babylon could be a future's name.

Quickly, with no preparation, hush,
Humility, the day dares dawn once more
In skies that hid in darkness at His star,
Veiled away their witness to His death.
Day at Tabor! Morning on the vines
Of Galilee, wind upon the wheat
Of Esdraelon! Dawn at Cana, Naim,
Gethsemane! Morning on the Hill
That gave forever morning to the world.

Not weary in the wear of ancient years,
Not stammering in syllables unsure
And half-forgotten, but alive and fresh
As this new day that breaks the casque of night,
His words are murmuring their plea above
A bread that learned here first obedience,
And over wine that dripped here in His blood
Before the nails were hammered in His Hands.
Calvary returns at Calvary.

Until the circling hours, set in the long
Succession of the hard two thousand years,
Move to Europe from the advent East
Whence the Cup came in the speech of Paul.
Sanctuaries brim that yet recall
They once were missioned out of Antioch.

Corinthians, Galatians, heirs to Titus,
Thessalonians, Timothy's
Blood brothers in the old advice, the kin
Of Philemon, Ephesians crowd the day.
Milan rehears Augustine's dialogue
With Ambrose spoken for a newer praise.

Europe is created of the Deed,
To wear Him like identity and claim
Across the quick divisionals that meet
At many borders, making one the whole
Rich difference, as though a single word
Had shattered into happy languages.
Alive with Consecrations, this is earth
That wavers under summoning of bells,
And everywhere the dawn strikes sleep to lift
Reopened Europe eyes to single hope.

Towns that are the sites of history
And saints keep village pride for names that thread
World litanies. Padua and Prague,
Budapest, Siena, Umbrian hills
Awake remembering, to follow streets
Like entrances that lead to daily shrines.
Monasteries chant beneath the cowls

To Tierce, and then in hooded silence, walk
Thanksgivings on the vowed unbarren stone.

Assisi, Florence, Mantua, Castile,
Toledo, Cracow, Reggio, and Rome.

Morning is a destiny at Rome,
A breath above the altars buried deep
In marble, tiered and banked and set among
The tombs, the catacombs, and over dust
Of witnesses that death is not for Rome,
Save His Whose death is Rome's unbroken life.

Sleeping in the night a man has lain
Who bears upon his heart the troubled dreams
Of all the world. He rises to the dawn,
And here at center, vaticaned, apart,
Sealed within a Name for history,
His voice is Peter's voice and on his face
Comes Peter's countenance.

                              Europe kneels
And is the gleaning multitude that takes
The more-than-manna that their fathers knew.

Searching altars on this wearied land,
Counting at the sunrise summoning,
We must be paused before a patch of earth
Like no other, and, as Golgotha,
Forever streaks in scar upon the earth.

The air still shivers in the memory
Of screams; whips still cut, bludgeons thud,
And gardens in posterity must leave
The stench, pervasive, and the soil will blanch
To blisters through a thousand years of seed.

Posts were bolted to electric gates;
Agony attempted to unman
The living man. Here once eight hundred priests
Were herded in a pen like branded kine.

There is a shack at Dachau with a plank
Nailed horizontal at a farther wall.
At midnight on a secret Christmas Eve
Eight hundred cupped their hands about a crumb

Of bread. They wore no vestments, sleeved no alb,
Lit no candles, touched no paten edge!

Crowded at the nude, the stolen plank,
A priest made Consecration; all the rest
Repeated in a unison of pain:
This, my Body; This, the chalice of my Blood.

The fields of France are widening to sun.

(Beauvais and Tours, Amiens, Sens,
Mont Saint Michel, Le Mans and Rheims,
The aisles of Chartres; doors of Notre Dame.)

London rises in the river's mist
To hear nostalgic bells from merry days.

The tended candles blaze in Ireland.

Today,
Or any day,

Is swift, thin folio to all of time,
A wheel that turns but to begin anew,
A moment, merely, an anonymous,
Brief, undistinguished passage of a dawn
Between all dawns, and yet . . . His silent quest
Rings a silver thunder round the world.
Breaking of the Hosts, the whisperings,
Throw His earth-storm pleading to the skies;
Peoples rising are like armies come
Of Malachias' promise, and the Bread
That is His Own is end of endless hunger.

Earth, the spinning earth, that reels through space,
Bleeds holy in His hands for all the earth
Is altar, and the altar lifts . . . . . . !